CONGRATULATIONS!
You are the
WINNER!

As a valued customer, you earned a special bonus from our team at Georgica's World. We want to thank you for choosing our book and to show our appreciation, we are giving you a **free** guide to the **5 best benefits of coloring** in **PDF** format. To **CLAIM** your bonus, scan the **QR CODE** on this page or visit **https://www.georgicasworld.com/magnet**.
Thank you for choosing Georgica's World; we look forward to serving you in the future.
But that's not all! Another **surprise** for you is a **FREE PDF** file containing engaging and fun coloring pages carefully chosen for you.
Download the guide and coloring pages and start using them today! We hope you enjoy these special bonuses and that they will help you get out of your daily routine.

or go to: **https://www.georgicasworld.com/magnet**

COOKING classes

This Book Belongs to:

____

____

Recipe 1 : _______________

PREP TIME

COOK TIME

COOK TEMP

FREEZING

○ yes   ○ no

SERVES

② ④ ⑥ ⑧ ⑩

DIFFICULTY

① ② ③ ④ ⑤

REVIEW

☆ ☆ ☆ ☆ ☆

VEGETARIAN ☐

DAIRY FREE ☐

LOW CARB ☐

GLUTEN FREE ☐

SUGAR FREE ☐

Ingredients:

Directions:

Notes:

Recipe 2 : ________________

PREP TIME ________________

COOK TIME ________________

COOK TEMP ________________

FREEZING

○ yes   ○ no

SERVES

② ④ ⑥ ⑧ ⑩

DIFFICULTY

① ② ③ ④ ⑤

REVIEW

☆ ☆ ☆ ☆ ☆

VEGETARIAN ☐

DAIRY FREE ☐

LOW CARB ☐

GLUTEN FREE ☐

SUGAR FREE ☐

Ingredients:

Directions:

Notes:

Recipe 3: _______________

PREP TIME _______

COOK TIME _______

COOK TEMP _______

FREEZING _______
◯ yes   ◯ no

SERVES _______
② ④ ⑥ ⑧ ⑩

DIFFICULTY _______
① ② ③ ④ ⑤

REVIEW _______
☆ ☆ ☆ ☆ ☆

VEGETARIAN ☐

DAIRY FREE ☐

LOW CARB ☐

GLUTEN FREE ☐

SUGAR FREE ☐

Ingredients:

Directions:

Notes:

Recipe 4: ___________

Ingredients:

PREP TIME

COOK TIME

COOK TEMP

FREEZING
◯ yes   ◯ no

SERVES
② ④ ⑥ ⑧ ⑩

DIFFICULTY
① ② ③ ④ ⑤

REVIEW
☆ ☆ ☆ ☆ ☆

VEGETARIAN ☐
DAIRY FREE ☐
LOW CARB ☐
GLUTEN FREE ☐
SUGAR FREE ☐

Directions:

Notes:

Recipe 5: _______________

PREP TIME

COOK TIME

COOK TEMP

FREEZING

◯ yes ◯ no

SERVES

② ④ ⑥ ⑧ ⑩

DIFFICULTY

① ② ③ ④ ⑤

REVIEW

☆ ☆ ☆ ☆ ☆

VEGETARIAN ☐

DAIRY FREE ☐

LOW CARB ☐

GLUTEN FREE ☐

SUGAR FREE ☐

Ingredients:

Directions:

Notes:

Recipe 6: _______________

PREP TIME

COOK TIME

COOK TEMP

FREEZING

◯ yes ◯ no

SERVES

② ④ ⑥ ⑧ ⑩

DIFFICULTY

① ② ③ ④ ⑤

REVIEW

☆ ☆ ☆ ☆ ☆

VEGETARIAN ☐

DAIRY FREE ☐

LOW CARB ☐

GLUTEN FREE ☐

SUGAR FREE ☐

Ingredients:

Directions:

Notes:

Recipe 7: _______________

PREP TIME

COOK TIME

COOK TEMP

FREEZING

◯ yes   ◯ no

SERVES

② ④ ⑥ ⑧ ⑩

DIFFICULTY

① ② ③ ④ ⑤

REVIEW

☆ ☆ ☆ ☆ ☆

VEGETARIAN ☐
DAIRY FREE ☐
LOW CARB ☐
GLUTEN FREE ☐
SUGAR FREE ☐

Ingredients:

Directions:

Notes:

Recipe 8: ______________________

PREP TIME

COOK TIME

COOK TEMP

FREEZING

◯ yes   ◯ no

SERVES

② ④ ⑥ ⑧ ⑩

DIFFICULTY

① ② ③ ④ ⑤

REVIEW

☆ ☆ ☆ ☆ ☆

VEGETARIAN ☐

DAIRY FREE ☐

LOW CARB ☐

GLUTEN FREE ☐

SUGAR FREE ☐

Ingredients:

Directions:

Notes:

Recipe 9: _______________

PREP TIME

COOK TIME

COOK TEMP

FREEZING

◯ yes   ◯ no

SERVES

② ④ ⑥ ⑧ ⑩

DIFFICULTY

① ② ③ ④ ⑤

REVIEW

☆ ☆ ☆ ☆ ☆

VEGETARIAN ☐

DAIRY FREE ☐

LOW CARB ☐

GLUTEN FREE ☐

SUGAR FREE ☐

Ingredients:

Directions:

Notes:

Recipe 10: _______________

PREP TIME

COOK TIME

COOK TEMP

FREEZING

◯ yes   ◯ no

SERVES

② ④ ⑥ ⑧ ⑩

DIFFICULTY

① ② ③ ④ ⑤

REVIEW

☆ ☆ ☆ ☆ ☆

VEGETARIAN ☐

DAIRY FREE ☐

LOW CARB ☐

GLUTEN FREE ☐

SUGAR FREE ☐

Ingredients:

Directions:

Notes:

Recipe 11: _______________

PREP TIME _______________

COOK TIME _______________

COOK TEMP _______________

FREEZING _______________

◯ yes   ◯ no

SERVES _______________

② ④ ⑥ ⑧ ⑩

DIFFICULTY _______________

① ② ③ ④ ⑤

REVIEW _______________

☆ ☆ ☆ ☆ ☆

VEGETARIAN ☐

DAIRY FREE ☐

LOW CARB ☐

GLUTEN FREE ☐

SUGAR FREE ☐

Ingredients:

Directions:

Notes:

Recipe 12: ___________________

PREP TIME

COOK TIME

COOK TEMP

FREEZING

◯ yes ◯ no

SERVES

② ④ ⑥ ⑧ ⑩

DIFFICULTY

① ② ③ ④ ⑤

REVIEW

☆ ☆ ☆ ☆ ☆

VEGETARIAN ☐

DAIRY FREE ☐

LOW CARB ☐

GLUTEN FREE ☐

SUGAR FREE ☐

Ingredients:

Directions:

Notes:

Recipe 13: ___________________

PREP TIME ___________

COOK TIME ___________

COOK TEMP ___________

FREEZING ___________
◯ yes   ◯ no

SERVES
② ④ ⑥ ⑧ ⑩

DIFFICULTY
① ② ③ ④ ⑤

REVIEW
☆ ☆ ☆ ☆ ☆

VEGETARIAN ☐
DAIRY FREE ☐
LOW CARB ☐
GLUTEN FREE ☐
SUGAR FREE ☐

Ingredients:

Directions:

Notes:

Recipe 14: ___________________

PREP TIME

COOK TIME

COOK TEMP

FREEZING

◯ yes   ◯ no

SERVES

② ④ ⑥ ⑧ ⑩

DIFFICULTY

① ② ③ ④ ⑤

REVIEW

☆ ☆ ☆ ☆ ☆

VEGETARIAN ☐

DAIRY FREE ☐

LOW CARB ☐

GLUTEN FREE ☐

SUGAR FREE ☐

Ingredients:

Directions:

Notes:

Recipe 15: _______________

PREP TIME _______

COOK TIME _______

COOK TEMP _______

FREEZING _______

○ yes ○ no

SERVES

② ④ ⑥ ⑧ ⑩

DIFFICULTY

① ② ③ ④ ⑤

REVIEW

☆ ☆ ☆ ☆ ☆

VEGETARIAN ☐

DAIRY FREE ☐

LOW CARB ☐

GLUTEN FREE ☐

SUGAR FREE ☐

Ingredients:

Directions:

Notes:

Recipe 16: ___________________

PREP TIME

COOK TIME

COOK TEMP

FREEZING

◯ yes   ◯ no

SERVES

② ④ ⑥ ⑧ ⑩

DIFFICULTY

① ② ③ ④ ⑤

REVIEW

☆ ☆ ☆ ☆ ☆

VEGETARIAN ☐

DAIRY FREE ☐

LOW CARB ☐

GLUTEN FREE ☐

SUGAR FREE ☐

Ingredients:

Directions:

Notes:

Recipe 17: _______________

Ingredients:

PREP TIME

COOK TIME

COOK TEMP

FREEZING

◯ yes ◯ no

SERVES

② ④ ⑥ ⑧ ⑩

DIFFICULTY

① ② ③ ④ ⑤

REVIEW

☆ ☆ ☆ ☆ ☆

VEGETARIAN ☐

DAIRY FREE ☐

LOW CARB ☐

GLUTEN FREE ☐

SUGAR FREE ☐

Directions:

Notes:

Recipe 18: ___________________

PREP TIME
____

COOK TIME
____

COOK TEMP
____

FREEZING

◯ yes   ◯ no

SERVES

② ④ ⑥ ⑧ ⑩

DIFFICULTY

① ② ③ ④ ⑤

REVIEW

☆ ☆ ☆ ☆ ☆

VEGETARIAN ☐

DAIRY FREE ☐

LOW CARB ☐

GLUTEN FREE ☐

SUGAR FREE ☐

Ingredients:

Directions:

Notes:

Recipe 19: _______________

PREP TIME

COOK TIME

COOK TEMP

FREEZING
◯ yes   ◯ no

SERVES
② ④ ⑥ ⑧ ⑩

DIFFICULTY
① ② ③ ④ ⑤

REVIEW
☆ ☆ ☆ ☆ ☆

VEGETARIAN ☐
DAIRY FREE ☐
LOW CARB ☐
GLUTEN FREE ☐
SUGAR FREE ☐

Ingredients:

Directions:

Notes:

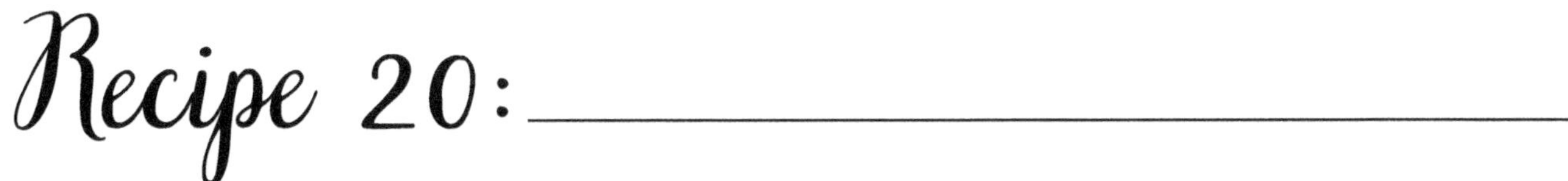

Recipe 20: _______________

PREP TIME
____

COOK TIME
____

COOK TEMP
____

FREEZING
◯ yes   ◯ no

SERVES
② ④ ⑥ ⑧ ⑩

DIFFICULTY
① ② ③ ④ ⑤

REVIEW
☆ ☆ ☆ ☆ ☆

VEGETARIAN ☐
DAIRY FREE ☐
LOW CARB ☐
GLUTEN FREE ☐
SUGAR FREE ☐

Ingredients:
____

Directions:
____

Notes:
____

Recipe 21: ___________________

PREP TIME

COOK TIME

COOK TEMP

FREEZING

◯ yes   ◯ no

SERVES

② ④ ⑥ ⑧ ⑩

DIFFICULTY

① ② ③ ④ ⑤

REVIEW

☆ ☆ ☆ ☆ ☆

VEGETARIAN ☐

DAIRY FREE ☐

LOW CARB ☐

GLUTEN FREE ☐

SUGAR FREE ☐

Ingredients:

Directions:

Notes:

Recipe 22:

PREP TIME

COOK TIME

COOK TEMP

FREEZING

◯ yes   ◯ no

SERVES

② ④ ⑥ ⑧ ⑩

DIFFICULTY

① ② ③ ④ ⑤

REVIEW

☆ ☆ ☆ ☆ ☆

VEGETARIAN ☐

DAIRY FREE ☐

LOW CARB ☐

GLUTEN FREE ☐

SUGAR FREE ☐

Ingredients:

Directions:

Notes:

Recipe 23:________________

PREP TIME

COOK TIME

COOK TEMP

FREEZING

◯ yes ◯ no

SERVES

② ④ ⑥ ⑧ ⑩

DIFFICULTY

① ② ③ ④ ⑤

REVIEW

☆ ☆ ☆ ☆ ☆

VEGETARIAN	☐
DAIRY FREE	☐
LOW CARB	☐
GLUTEN FREE	☐
SUGAR FREE	☐

Ingredients:

Directions:

Notes:

Recipe 24: ___________________

PREP TIME

COOK TIME

COOK TEMP

FREEZING

◯ yes   ◯ no

SERVES

② ④ ⑥ ⑧ ⑩

DIFFICULTY

① ② ③ ④ ⑤

REVIEW

☆ ☆ ☆ ☆ ☆

VEGETARIAN ☐

DAIRY FREE ☐

LOW CARB ☐

GLUTEN FREE ☐

SUGAR FREE ☐

Ingredients:

Directions:

Notes:

Recipe 25: _______________

PREP TIME

COOK TIME

COOK TEMP

FREEZING

◯ yes   ◯ no

SERVES

② ④ ⑥ ⑧ ⑩

DIFFICULTY

① ② ③ ④ ⑤

REVIEW

☆ ☆ ☆ ☆ ☆

VEGETARIAN ☐

DAIRY FREE ☐

LOW CARB ☐

GLUTEN FREE ☐

SUGAR FREE ☐

Ingredients:

Directions:

Notes:

Recipe 26: _______________

PREP TIME

COOK TIME

COOK TEMP

FREEZING

◯ yes   ◯ no

SERVES

② ④ ⑥ ⑧ ⑩

DIFFICULTY

① ② ③ ④ ⑤

REVIEW

☆ ☆ ☆ ☆ ☆

VEGETARIAN	☐
DAIRY FREE	☐
LOW CARB	☐
GLUTEN FREE	☐
SUGAR FREE	☐

Ingredients:

Directions:

Notes:

Recipe 27:___________________

PREP TIME

COOK TIME

COOK TEMP

FREEZING
◯ yes   ◯ no

SERVES
② ④ ⑥ ⑧ ⑩

DIFFICULTY
① ② ③ ④ ⑤

REVIEW
☆ ☆ ☆ ☆ ☆

VEGETARIAN ☐
DAIRY FREE ☐
LOW CARB ☐
GLUTEN FREE ☐
SUGAR FREE ☐

Ingredients:

Directions:

Notes:

Recipe 28: _______________

PREP TIME

COOK TIME

COOK TEMP

FREEZING

◯ yes   ◯ no

SERVES

② ④ ⑥ ⑧ ⑩

DIFFICULTY

① ② ③ ④ ⑤

REVIEW

☆ ☆ ☆ ☆ ☆

VEGETARIAN ☐

DAIRY FREE ☐

LOW CARB ☐

GLUTEN FREE ☐

SUGAR FREE ☐

Ingredients:

Directions:

Notes:

Recipe 29: ______________________

PREP TIME

COOK TIME

COOK TEMP

FREEZING

◯ yes   ◯ no

SERVES

② ④ ⑥ ⑧ ⑩

DIFFICULTY

① ② ③ ④ ⑤

REVIEW

☆ ☆ ☆ ☆ ☆

VEGETARIAN ☐
DAIRY FREE ☐
LOW CARB ☐
GLUTEN FREE ☐
SUGAR FREE ☐

Ingredients:

Directions:

Notes:

Recipe 30: _______________

PREP TIME

COOK TIME

COOK TEMP

FREEZING

◯ yes ◯ no

SERVES

② ④ ⑥ ⑧ ⑩

DIFFICULTY

① ② ③ ④ ⑤

REVIEW

☆ ☆ ☆ ☆ ☆

VEGETARIAN ☐

DAIRY FREE ☐

LOW CARB ☐

GLUTEN FREE ☐

SUGAR FREE ☐

Ingredients:

Directions:

Notes:

Recipe 31: _______________

PREP TIME _______________

COOK TIME _______________

COOK TEMP _______________

FREEZING _______________

◯ yes ◯ no

SERVES _______________

② ④ ⑥ ⑧ ⑩

DIFFICULTY _______________

① ② ③ ④ ⑤

REVIEW _______________

☆ ☆ ☆ ☆ ☆

VEGETARIAN ☐

DAIRY FREE ☐

LOW CARB ☐

GLUTEN FREE ☐

SUGAR FREE ☐

Ingredients:

Directions:

Notes:

Recipe 32: _______________

PREP TIME

COOK TIME

COOK TEMP

FREEZING

◯ yes   ◯ no

SERVES

② ④ ⑥ ⑧ ⑩

DIFFICULTY

① ② ③ ④ ⑤

REVIEW

☆ ☆ ☆ ☆ ☆

VEGETARIAN ☐

DAIRY FREE ☐

LOW CARB ☐

GLUTEN FREE ☐

SUGAR FREE ☐

Ingredients:

Directions:

Notes:

Recipe 33:

PREP TIME

COOK TIME

COOK TEMP

FREEZING

◯ yes   ◯ no

SERVES

② ④ ⑥ ⑧ ⑩

DIFFICULTY

① ② ③ ④ ⑤

REVIEW

☆ ☆ ☆ ☆ ☆

VEGETARIAN ☐
DAIRY FREE ☐
LOW CARB ☐
GLUTEN FREE ☐
SUGAR FREE ☐

Ingredients:

Directions:

Notes:

Recipe 34: _______________

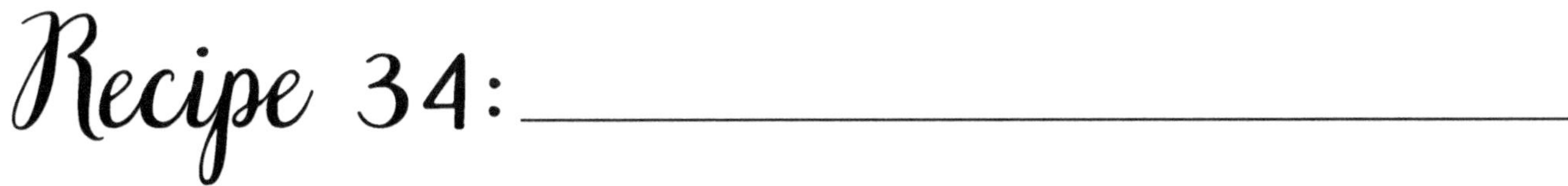

PREP TIME

COOK TIME

COOK TEMP

FREEZING

◯ yes   ◯ no

SERVES

② ④ ⑥ ⑧ ⑩

DIFFICULTY

① ② ③ ④ ⑤

REVIEW

☆ ☆ ☆ ☆ ☆

VEGETARIAN ☐

DAIRY FREE ☐

LOW CARB ☐

GLUTEN FREE ☐

SUGAR FREE ☐

Ingredients:

Directions:

Notes:

Recipe 35: _______________

PREP TIME

COOK TIME

COOK TEMP

FREEZING

◯ yes   ◯ no

SERVES

② ④ ⑥ ⑧ ⑩

DIFFICULTY

① ② ③ ④ ⑤

REVIEW

☆ ☆ ☆ ☆ ☆

VEGETARIAN ☐

DAIRY FREE ☐

LOW CARB ☐

GLUTEN FREE ☐

SUGAR FREE ☐

Ingredients:

Directions:

Notes:

Recipe 36: _______________

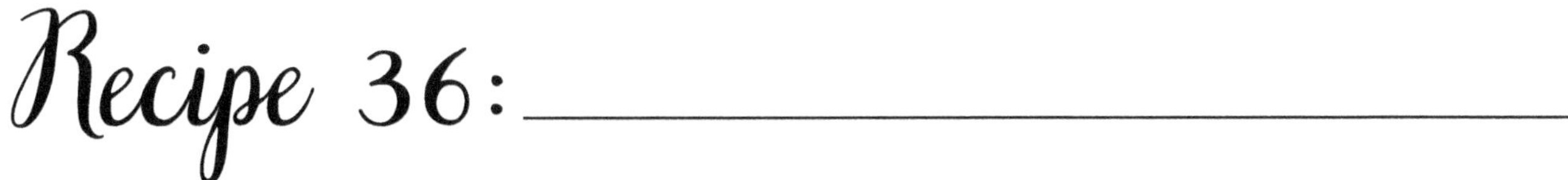

PREP TIME

COOK TIME

COOK TEMP

FREEZING

◯ yes   ◯ no

SERVES

② ④ ⑥ ⑧ ⑩

DIFFICULTY

① ② ③ ④ ⑤

REVIEW

☆ ☆ ☆ ☆ ☆

VEGETARIAN	☐
DAIRY FREE	☐
LOW CARB	☐
GLUTEN FREE	☐
SUGAR FREE	☐

Ingredients:

Directions:

Notes:

Recipe 37:______________________

PREP TIME

COOK TIME

COOK TEMP

FREEZING

◯ yes   ◯ no

SERVES

② ④ ⑥ ⑧ ⑩

DIFFICULTY

① ② ③ ④ ⑤

REVIEW

☆ ☆ ☆ ☆ ☆

VEGETARIAN ☐
DAIRY FREE ☐
LOW CARB ☐
GLUTEN FREE ☐
SUGAR FREE ☐

Ingredients:

Directions:

Notes:

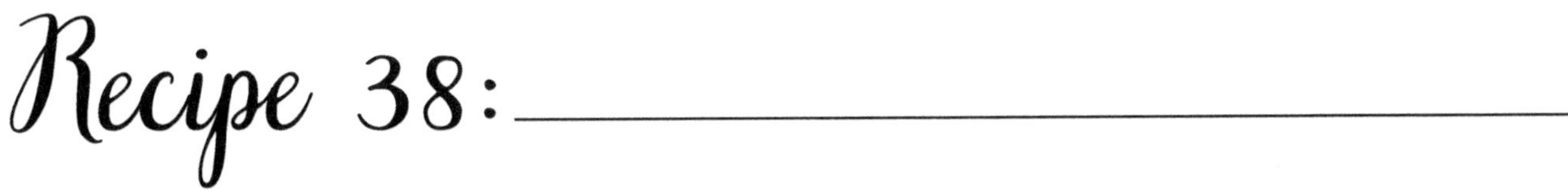

Recipe 38:

PREP TIME

COOK TIME

COOK TEMP

FREEZING

◯ yes   ◯ no

SERVES

② ④ ⑥ ⑧ ⑩

DIFFICULTY

① ② ③ ④ ⑤

REVIEW

☆ ☆ ☆ ☆ ☆

VEGETARIAN ☐

DAIRY FREE ☐

LOW CARB ☐

GLUTEN FREE ☐

SUGAR FREE ☐

Ingredients:

Directions:

Notes:

Recipe 39: _______________

PREP TIME ________

COOK TIME ________

COOK TEMP ________

FREEZING

◯ yes   ◯ no

SERVES

② ④ ⑥ ⑧ ⑩

DIFFICULTY

① ② ③ ④ ⑤

REVIEW

☆ ☆ ☆ ☆ ☆

VEGETARIAN ☐

DAIRY FREE ☐

LOW CARB ☐

GLUTEN FREE ☐

SUGAR FREE ☐

Ingredients:

Directions:

Notes:

Recipe 40: ________________

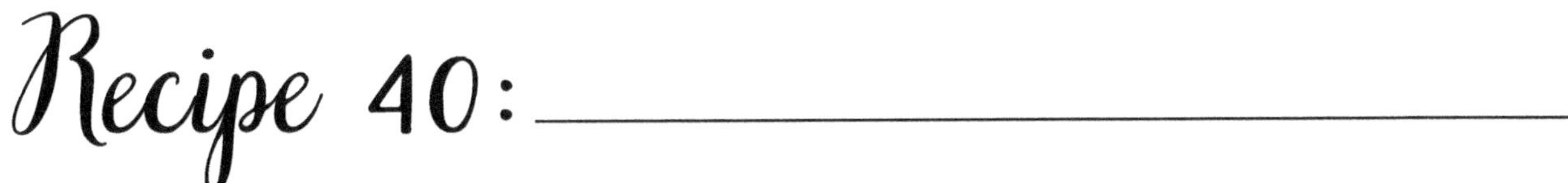

PREP TIME ________

COOK TIME ________

COOK TEMP ________

FREEZING
◯ yes   ◯ no

SERVES
② ④ ⑥ ⑧ ⑩

DIFFICULTY
① ② ③ ④ ⑤

REVIEW
☆ ☆ ☆ ☆ ☆

VEGETARIAN ☐
DAIRY FREE ☐
LOW CARB ☐
GLUTEN FREE ☐
SUGAR FREE ☐

Ingredients:
____

Directions:
____

Notes:
____

Recipe 41: _______________

PREP TIME

COOK TIME

COOK TEMP

FREEZING

◯ yes   ◯ no

SERVES

② ④ ⑥ ⑧ ⑩

DIFFICULTY

① ② ③ ④ ⑤

REVIEW

☆ ☆ ☆ ☆ ☆

VEGETARIAN ☐

DAIRY FREE ☐

LOW CARB ☐

GLUTEN FREE ☐

SUGAR FREE ☐

Ingredients:

Directions:

Notes:

Recipe 42:

PREP TIME

COOK TIME

COOK TEMP

FREEZING

○ yes   ○ no

SERVES

② ④ ⑥ ⑧ ⑩

DIFFICULTY

① ② ③ ④ ⑤

REVIEW

☆ ☆ ☆ ☆ ☆

VEGETARIAN ☐

DAIRY FREE ☐

LOW CARB ☐

GLUTEN FREE ☐

SUGAR FREE ☐

Ingredients:

Directions:

Notes:

Recipe 43: _______________

PREP TIME

COOK TIME

COOK TEMP

FREEZING

◯ yes   ◯ no

SERVES

② ④ ⑥ ⑧ ⑩

DIFFICULTY

① ② ③ ④ ⑤

REVIEW

☆ ☆ ☆ ☆ ☆

VEGETARIAN ☐

DAIRY FREE ☐

LOW CARB ☐

GLUTEN FREE ☐

SUGAR FREE ☐

Ingredients:

Directions:

Notes:

Recipe 44: _______________

PREP TIME

COOK TIME

COOK TEMP

FREEZING

◯ yes   ◯ no

SERVES

② ④ ⑥ ⑧ ⑩

DIFFICULTY

① ② ③ ④ ⑤

REVIEW

☆ ☆ ☆ ☆ ☆

VEGETARIAN ☐

DAIRY FREE ☐

LOW CARB ☐

GLUTEN FREE ☐

SUGAR FREE ☐

Ingredients:

Directions:

Notes:

Recipe 45: _______________

PREP TIME

COOK TIME

COOK TEMP

FREEZING

◯ yes   ◯ no

SERVES

② ④ ⑥ ⑧ ⑩

DIFFICULTY

① ② ③ ④ ⑤

REVIEW

☆ ☆ ☆ ☆ ☆

VEGETARIAN ☐

DAIRY FREE ☐

LOW CARB ☐

GLUTEN FREE ☐

SUGAR FREE ☐

Ingredients:

Directions:

Notes:

SCAN this **QR** code to
DISCOVER ALL OUR BOOKS

Recipe 46: _______________

PREP TIME

COOK TIME

COOK TEMP

FREEZING

◯ yes   ◯ no

SERVES

② ④ ⑥ ⑧ ⑩

DIFFICULTY

① ② ③ ④ ⑤

REVIEW

☆ ☆ ☆ ☆ ☆

VEGETARIAN ☐

DAIRY FREE ☐

LOW CARB ☐

GLUTEN FREE ☐

SUGAR FREE ☐

Ingredients:

Directions:

Notes:

Recipe 47: _______________

PREP TIME

COOK TIME

COOK TEMP

FREEZING
◯ yes   ◯ no

SERVES
② ④ ⑥ ⑧ ⑩

DIFFICULTY
① ② ③ ④ ⑤

REVIEW
☆ ☆ ☆ ☆ ☆

VEGETARIAN ☐
DAIRY FREE ☐
LOW CARB ☐
GLUTEN FREE ☐
SUGAR FREE ☐

Ingredients:

Directions:

Notes:

Recipe 48: _______________

PREP TIME _______________

COOK TIME _______________

COOK TEMP _______________

FREEZING _______________
◯ yes   ◯ no

SERVES
② ④ ⑥ ⑧ ⑩

DIFFICULTY
① ② ③ ④ ⑤

REVIEW
☆ ☆ ☆ ☆ ☆

VEGETARIAN ☐
DAIRY FREE ☐
LOW CARB ☐
GLUTEN FREE ☐
SUGAR FREE ☐

Ingredients:

Directions:

Notes:

Recipe 49: _______________

PREP TIME

COOK TIME

COOK TEMP

FREEZING

◯ yes   ◯ no

SERVES

② ④ ⑥ ⑧ ⑩

DIFFICULTY

① ② ③ ④ ⑤

REVIEW

☆ ☆ ☆ ☆ ☆

VEGETARIAN ☐

DAIRY FREE ☐

LOW CARB ☐

GLUTEN FREE ☐

SUGAR FREE ☐

Ingredients:

Directions:

Notes:

Recipe 50: _______________

PREP TIME ______

COOK TIME ______

COOK TEMP ______

FREEZING ______

◯ yes   ◯ no

SERVES ______

② ④ ⑥ ⑧ ⑩

DIFFICULTY ______

① ② ③ ④ ⑤

REVIEW ______

☆ ☆ ☆ ☆ ☆

VEGETARIAN	☐
DAIRY FREE	☐
LOW CARB	☐
GLUTEN FREE	☐
SUGAR FREE	☐

Ingredients:

_______________ _______________

_______________ _______________

_______________ _______________

_______________ _______________

_______________ _______________

Directions:

____

____

____

____

____

____

____

____

____

Notes:

____

____

____

____

Recipe 51: _______________

PREP TIME

COOK TIME

COOK TEMP

FREEZING
◯ yes   ◯ no

SERVES
② ④ ⑥ ⑧ ⑩

DIFFICULTY
① ② ③ ④ ⑤

REVIEW
☆ ☆ ☆ ☆ ☆

VEGETARIAN ☐
DAIRY FREE ☐
LOW CARB ☐
GLUTEN FREE ☐
SUGAR FREE ☐

Ingredients:

Directions:

Notes:

Recipe 52: _______________

PREP TIME

COOK TIME

COOK TEMP

FREEZING

◯ yes   ◯ no

SERVES

② ④ ⑥ ⑧ ⑩

DIFFICULTY

① ② ③ ④ ⑤

REVIEW

☆ ☆ ☆ ☆ ☆

VEGETARIAN ☐

DAIRY FREE ☐

LOW CARB ☐

GLUTEN FREE ☐

SUGAR FREE ☐

Ingredients:

Directions:

Notes:

Recipe 53: _______________

PREP TIME ______

COOK TIME ______

COOK TEMP ______

FREEZING ______
◯ yes   ◯ no

SERVES ______
② ④ ⑥ ⑧ ⑩

DIFFICULTY ______
① ② ③ ④ ⑤

REVIEW ______
☆ ☆ ☆ ☆ ☆

VEGETARIAN ☐

DAIRY FREE ☐

LOW CARB ☐

GLUTEN FREE ☐

SUGAR FREE ☐

Ingredients:

Directions:

Notes:

Recipe 54: _______________

<table>
<tr><td>

PREP TIME ______

COOK TIME ______

COOK TEMP ______

FREEZING ______
◯ yes   ◯ no

SERVES ______
② ④ ⑥ ⑧ ⑩

DIFFICULTY ______
① ② ③ ④ ⑤

REVIEW ______
☆ ☆ ☆ ☆ ☆

VEGETARIAN ☐
DAIRY FREE ☐
LOW CARB ☐
GLUTEN FREE ☐
SUGAR FREE ☐

</td></tr>
</table>

Ingredients:

Directions:

Notes:

Recipe 55: _______________

PREP TIME _______

COOK TIME _______

COOK TEMP _______

FREEZING
◯ yes   ◯ no

SERVES
② ④ ⑥ ⑧ ⑩

DIFFICULTY
① ② ③ ④ ⑤

REVIEW
☆ ☆ ☆ ☆ ☆

VEGETARIAN ☐
DAIRY FREE ☐
LOW CARB ☐
GLUTEN FREE ☐
SUGAR FREE ☐

Ingredients:

Directions:

Notes:

Recipe 56: _______________

PREP TIME

COOK TIME

COOK TEMP

FREEZING

◯ yes ◯ no

SERVES

② ④ ⑥ ⑧ ⑩

DIFFICULTY

① ② ③ ④ ⑤

REVIEW

☆ ☆ ☆ ☆ ☆

VEGETARIAN ☐

DAIRY FREE ☐

LOW CARB ☐

GLUTEN FREE ☐

SUGAR FREE ☐

Ingredients:

Directions:

Notes:

Recipe 57:_______________

PREP TIME

COOK TIME

COOK TEMP

FREEZING

◯ yes   ◯ no

SERVES

② ④ ⑥ ⑧ ⑩

DIFFICULTY

① ② ③ ④ ⑤

REVIEW

☆ ☆ ☆ ☆ ☆

VEGETARIAN ☐

DAIRY FREE ☐

LOW CARB ☐

GLUTEN FREE ☐

SUGAR FREE ☐

Ingredients:

Directions:

Notes:

Recipe 58: _______________

Ingredients:

Directions:

Notes:

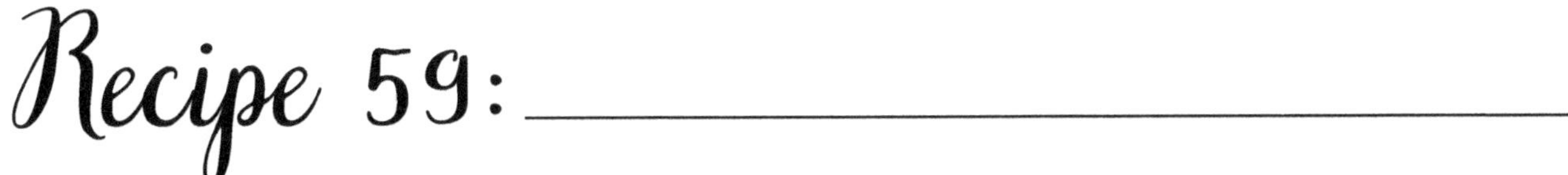

Recipe 59: _______________

PREP TIME ______

COOK TIME ______

COOK TEMP ______

FREEZING ______
◯ yes   ◯ no

SERVES ______
② ④ ⑥ ⑧ ⑩

DIFFICULTY ______
① ② ③ ④ ⑤

REVIEW ______
☆ ☆ ☆ ☆ ☆

VEGETARIAN ☐
DAIRY FREE ☐
LOW CARB ☐
GLUTEN FREE ☐
SUGAR FREE ☐

Ingredients:

Directions:

Notes:

Recipe 60: ________________

PREP TIME ________________

COOK TIME ________________

COOK TEMP ________________

FREEZING
◯ yes   ◯ no

SERVES
② ④ ⑥ ⑧ ⑩

DIFFICULTY
① ② ③ ④ ⑤

REVIEW
☆ ☆ ☆ ☆ ☆

VEGETARIAN ☐
DAIRY FREE ☐
LOW CARB ☐
GLUTEN FREE ☐
SUGAR FREE ☐

Ingredients:

Directions:

Notes:

Recipe 61: _______________

PREP TIME

COOK TIME

COOK TEMP

FREEZING

◯ yes   ◯ no

SERVES

② ④ ⑥ ⑧ ⑩

DIFFICULTY

① ② ③ ④ ⑤

REVIEW

☆ ☆ ☆ ☆ ☆

VEGETARIAN ☐

DAIRY FREE ☐

LOW CARB ☐

GLUTEN FREE ☐

SUGAR FREE ☐

Ingredients:

Directions:

Notes:

Recipe 62:

PREP TIME

COOK TIME

COOK TEMP

FREEZING

◯ yes   ◯ no

SERVES

② ④ ⑥ ⑧ ⑩

DIFFICULTY

① ② ③ ④ ⑤

REVIEW

☆ ☆ ☆ ☆ ☆

VEGETARIAN ☐

DAIRY FREE ☐

LOW CARB ☐

GLUTEN FREE ☐

SUGAR FREE ☐

Ingredients:

Directions:

Notes:

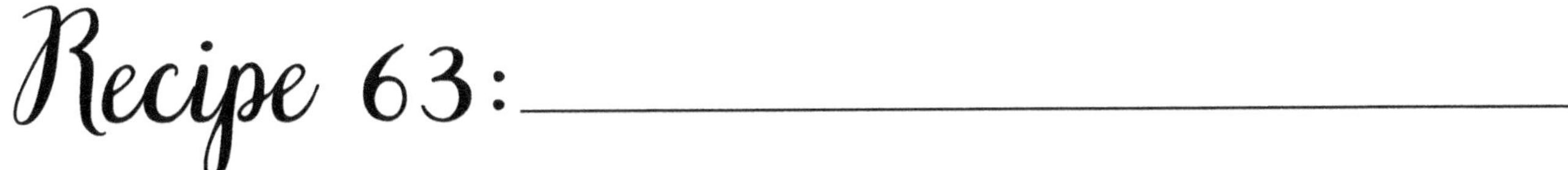

Recipe 63:

PREP TIME

COOK TIME

COOK TEMP

FREEZING

◯ yes   ◯ no

SERVES

② ④ ⑥ ⑧ ⑩

DIFFICULTY

① ② ③ ④ ⑤

REVIEW

☆ ☆ ☆ ☆ ☆

VEGETARIAN ☐

DAIRY FREE ☐

LOW CARB ☐

GLUTEN FREE ☐

SUGAR FREE ☐

Ingredients:

Directions:

Notes:

Recipe 64: _______________

PREP TIME

COOK TIME

COOK TEMP

FREEZING

◯ yes　◯ no

SERVES

②　④　⑥　⑧　⑩

DIFFICULTY

①　②　③　④　⑤

REVIEW

☆ ☆ ☆ ☆ ☆

VEGETARIAN ☐

DAIRY FREE ☐

LOW CARB ☐

GLUTEN FREE ☐

SUGAR FREE ☐

Ingredients:

Directions:

Notes:

Recipe 65: _______________

<u>PREP TIME</u>

<u>COOK TIME</u>

<u>COOK TEMP</u>

<u>FREEZING</u>
◯ yes   ◯ no

<u>SERVES</u>
② ④ ⑥ ⑧ ⑩

<u>DIFFICULTY</u>
① ② ③ ④ ⑤

<u>REVIEW</u>
☆ ☆ ☆ ☆ ☆

VEGETARIAN ☐
DAIRY FREE ☐
LOW CARB ☐
GLUTEN FREE ☐
SUGAR FREE ☐

Ingredients:

Directions:

Notes:

Recipe 66: ______________________

PREP TIME

COOK TIME

COOK TEMP

FREEZING

◯ yes   ◯ no

SERVES

② ④ ⑥ ⑧ ⑩

DIFFICULTY

① ② ③ ④ ⑤

REVIEW

☆ ☆ ☆ ☆ ☆

VEGETARIAN ☐

DAIRY FREE ☐

LOW CARB ☐

GLUTEN FREE ☐

SUGAR FREE ☐

Ingredients:

Directions:

Notes:

Recipe 67:

PREP TIME

COOK TIME

COOK TEMP

FREEZING

◯ yes ◯ no

SERVES

② ④ ⑥ ⑧ ⑩

DIFFICULTY

① ② ③ ④ ⑤

REVIEW

☆ ☆ ☆ ☆ ☆

VEGETARIAN ☐

DAIRY FREE ☐

LOW CARB ☐

GLUTEN FREE ☐

SUGAR FREE ☐

Ingredients:

Directions:

Notes:

Recipe 68: ___________________

PREP TIME ___________

COOK TIME ___________

COOK TEMP ___________

FREEZING ___________
◯ yes ◯ no

SERVES ___________
② ④ ⑥ ⑧ ⑩

DIFFICULTY ___________
① ② ③ ④ ⑤

REVIEW ___________
☆ ☆ ☆ ☆ ☆

VEGETARIAN ☐
DAIRY FREE ☐
LOW CARB ☐
GLUTEN FREE ☐
SUGAR FREE ☐

Ingredients:

Directions:

Notes:

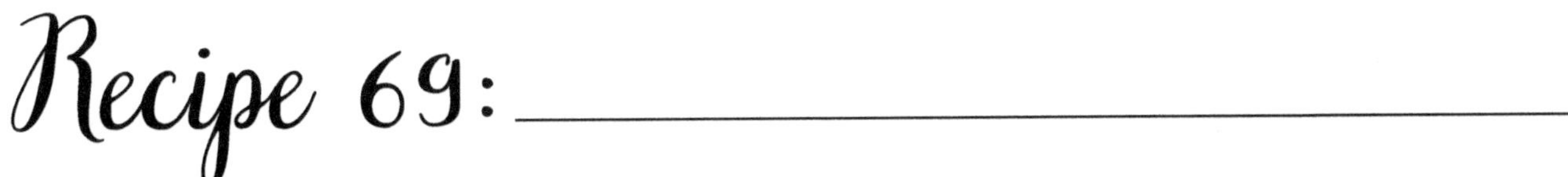

Recipe 69: _______________

PREP TIME

COOK TIME

COOK TEMP

FREEZING

◯ yes   ◯ no

SERVES

② ④ ⑥ ⑧ ⑩

DIFFICULTY

① ② ③ ④ ⑤

REVIEW

☆ ☆ ☆ ☆ ☆

VEGETARIAN ☐
DAIRY FREE ☐
LOW CARB ☐
GLUTEN FREE ☐
SUGAR FREE ☐

Ingredients:

Directions:

Notes:

Recipe 70:

PREP TIME

COOK TIME

COOK TEMP

FREEZING
◯ yes   ◯ no

SERVES
② ④ ⑥ ⑧ ⑩

DIFFICULTY
① ② ③ ④ ⑤

REVIEW
☆ ☆ ☆ ☆ ☆

VEGETARIAN ☐
DAIRY FREE ☐
LOW CARB ☐
GLUTEN FREE ☐
SUGAR FREE ☐

Ingredients:

Directions:

Notes:

Recipe 71: _______________

PREP TIME _______________

COOK TIME _______________

COOK TEMP _______________

FREEZING _______________
◯ yes   ◯ no

SERVES
② ④ ⑥ ⑧ ⑩

DIFFICULTY
① ② ③ ④ ⑤

REVIEW
☆ ☆ ☆ ☆ ☆

VEGETARIAN ☐
DAIRY FREE ☐
LOW CARB ☐
GLUTEN FREE ☐
SUGAR FREE ☐

Ingredients: _______________

Directions: _______________

Notes: _______________

Recipe 72:

PREP TIME

COOK TIME

COOK TEMP

FREEZING

◯ yes ◯ no

SERVES

② ④ ⑥ ⑧ ⑩

DIFFICULTY

① ② ③ ④ ⑤

REVIEW

☆ ☆ ☆ ☆ ☆

VEGETARIAN ☐
DAIRY FREE ☐
LOW CARB ☐
GLUTEN FREE ☐
SUGAR FREE ☐

Ingredients:

Directions:

Notes:

Recipe 73:

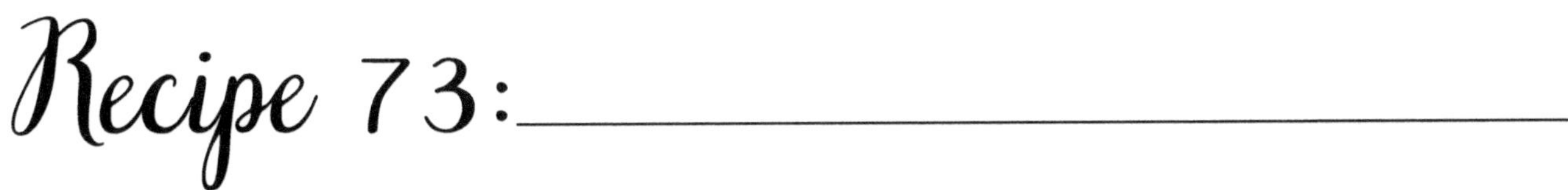

PREP TIME

COOK TIME

COOK TEMP

FREEZING
○ yes ○ no

SERVES
② ④ ⑥ ⑧ ⑩

DIFFICULTY
① ② ③ ④ ⑤

REVIEW
☆ ☆ ☆ ☆ ☆

VEGETARIAN ☐
DAIRY FREE ☐
LOW CARB ☐
GLUTEN FREE ☐
SUGAR FREE ☐

Ingredients:

Directions:

Notes:

Recipe 74: _______________

PREP TIME

COOK TIME

COOK TEMP

FREEZING

◯ yes   ◯ no

SERVES

② ④ ⑥ ⑧ ⑩

DIFFICULTY

① ② ③ ④ ⑤

REVIEW

☆ ☆ ☆ ☆ ☆

VEGETARIAN ☐

DAIRY FREE ☐

LOW CARB ☐

GLUTEN FREE ☐

SUGAR FREE ☐

Ingredients:

Directions:

Notes:

Recipe 75:______________________

PREP TIME

COOK TIME

COOK TEMP

FREEZING

○ yes   ○ no

SERVES

② ④ ⑥ ⑧ ⑩

DIFFICULTY

① ② ③ ④ ⑤

REVIEW

☆ ☆ ☆ ☆ ☆

VEGETARIAN ☐

DAIRY FREE ☐

LOW CARB ☐

GLUTEN FREE ☐

SUGAR FREE ☐

Ingredients:

Directions:

Notes:

Recipe 76: _______________

PREP TIME

COOK TIME

COOK TEMP

FREEZING

◯ yes ◯ no

SERVES

② ④ ⑥ ⑧ ⑩

DIFFICULTY

① ② ③ ④ ⑤

REVIEW

☆ ☆ ☆ ☆ ☆

VEGETARIAN ☐
DAIRY FREE ☐
LOW CARB ☐
GLUTEN FREE ☐
SUGAR FREE ☐

Ingredients:

Directions:

Notes:

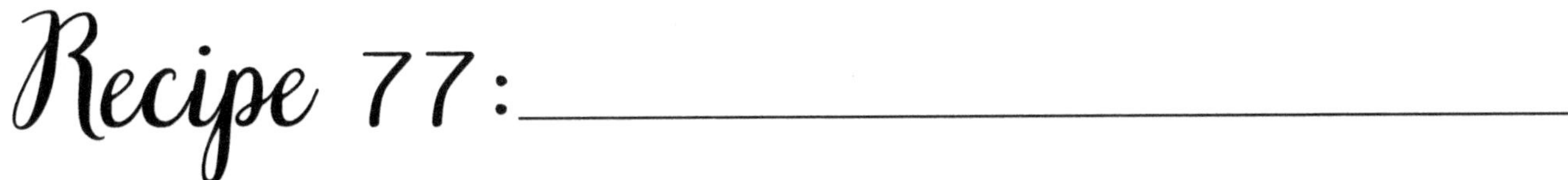

Recipe 77:______________

PREP TIME

COOK TIME

COOK TEMP

FREEZING

◯ yes ◯ no

SERVES

② ④ ⑥ ⑧ ⑩

DIFFICULTY

① ② ③ ④ ⑤

REVIEW

☆ ☆ ☆ ☆ ☆

VEGETARIAN ☐

DAIRY FREE ☐

LOW CARB ☐

GLUTEN FREE ☐

SUGAR FREE ☐

Ingredients:

Directions:

Notes:

Recipe 78: _______________

PREP TIME

COOK TIME

COOK TEMP

FREEZING

◯ yes ◯ no

SERVES

② ④ ⑥ ⑧ ⑩

DIFFICULTY

① ② ③ ④ ⑤

REVIEW

☆ ☆ ☆ ☆ ☆

VEGETARIAN ☐

DAIRY FREE ☐

LOW CARB ☐

GLUTEN FREE ☐

SUGAR FREE ☐

Ingredients:

Directions:

Notes:

Recipe 79: _______________

PREP TIME

COOK TIME

COOK TEMP

FREEZING

◯ yes   ◯ no

SERVES

② ④ ⑥ ⑧ ⑩

DIFFICULTY

① ② ③ ④ ⑤

REVIEW

☆ ☆ ☆ ☆ ☆

VEGETARIAN ☐

DAIRY FREE ☐

LOW CARB ☐

GLUTEN FREE ☐

SUGAR FREE ☐

Ingredients:

Directions:

Notes:

Recipe 80: _______________

PREP TIME

COOK TIME

COOK TEMP

FREEZING

◯ yes   ◯ no

SERVES

② ④ ⑥ ⑧ ⑩

DIFFICULTY

① ② ③ ④ ⑤

REVIEW

☆ ☆ ☆ ☆ ☆

VEGETARIAN ☐
DAIRY FREE ☐
LOW CARB ☐
GLUTEN FREE ☐
SUGAR FREE ☐

Ingredients:

Directions:

Notes:

Recipe 81: _______________

PREP TIME

COOK TIME

COOK TEMP

FREEZING

◯ yes   ◯ no

SERVES

② ④ ⑥ ⑧ ⑩

DIFFICULTY

① ② ③ ④ ⑤

REVIEW

☆ ☆ ☆ ☆ ☆

VEGETARIAN ☐

DAIRY FREE ☐

LOW CARB ☐

GLUTEN FREE ☐

SUGAR FREE ☐

Ingredients:

Directions:

Notes:

Recipe 82:

PREP TIME

COOK TIME

COOK TEMP

FREEZING

◯ yes   ◯ no

SERVES

② ④ ⑥ ⑧ ⑩

DIFFICULTY

① ② ③ ④ ⑤

REVIEW

☆ ☆ ☆ ☆ ☆

VEGETARIAN ☐
DAIRY FREE ☐
LOW CARB ☐
GLUTEN FREE ☐
SUGAR FREE ☐

Ingredients:

Directions:

Notes:

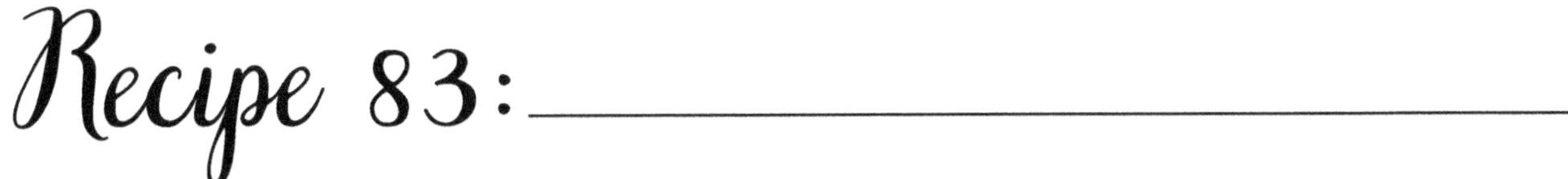

Recipe 83: _______________

PREP TIME

COOK TIME

COOK TEMP

FREEZING

◯ yes ◯ no

SERVES

② ④ ⑥ ⑧ ⑩

DIFFICULTY

① ② ③ ④ ⑤

REVIEW

☆ ☆ ☆ ☆ ☆

VEGETARIAN ☐

DAIRY FREE ☐

LOW CARB ☐

GLUTEN FREE ☐

SUGAR FREE ☐

Ingredients:

Directions:

Notes:

Recipe 84: _______________

PREP TIME

COOK TIME

COOK TEMP

FREEZING

○ yes   ○ no

SERVES

② ④ ⑥ ⑧ ⑩

DIFFICULTY

① ② ③ ④ ⑤

REVIEW

☆ ☆ ☆ ☆ ☆

VEGETARIAN ☐

DAIRY FREE ☐

LOW CARB ☐

GLUTEN FREE ☐

SUGAR FREE ☐

Ingredients:

Directions:

Notes:

Recipe 85: _______________

PREP TIME ___________

COOK TIME ___________

COOK TEMP ___________

FREEZING

◯ yes   ◯ no

SERVES

② ④ ⑥ ⑧ ⑩

DIFFICULTY

① ② ③ ④ ⑤

REVIEW

☆ ☆ ☆ ☆ ☆

VEGETARIAN ☐

DAIRY FREE ☐

LOW CARB ☐

GLUTEN FREE ☐

SUGAR FREE ☐

Ingredients:

Directions:

Notes:

Recipe 86: _______________

PREP TIME ___________

COOK TIME ___________

COOK TEMP ___________

FREEZING ___________

◯ yes   ◯ no

SERVES ___________

② ④ ⑥ ⑧ ⑩

DIFFICULTY ___________

① ② ③ ④ ⑤

REVIEW ___________

☆ ☆ ☆ ☆ ☆

VEGETARIAN ☐

DAIRY FREE ☐

LOW CARB ☐

GLUTEN FREE ☐

SUGAR FREE ☐

Ingredients:

Directions:

Notes:

Recipe 87:

PREP TIME

COOK TIME

COOK TEMP

FREEZING

◯ yes   ◯ no

SERVES

② ④ ⑥ ⑧ ⑩

DIFFICULTY

① ② ③ ④ ⑤

REVIEW

☆ ☆ ☆ ☆ ☆

VEGETARIAN ☐

DAIRY FREE ☐

LOW CARB ☐

GLUTEN FREE ☐

SUGAR FREE ☐

Ingredients:

Directions:

Notes:

Recipe 88: _______________

PREP TIME

COOK TIME

COOK TEMP

FREEZING

◯ yes   ◯ no

SERVES

② ④ ⑥ ⑧ ⑩

DIFFICULTY

① ② ③ ④ ⑤

REVIEW

☆ ☆ ☆ ☆ ☆

VEGETARIAN ☐

DAIRY FREE ☐

LOW CARB ☐

GLUTEN FREE ☐

SUGAR FREE ☐

Ingredients:

Directions:

Notes:

Recipe 89: _______________

Ingredients:

Directions:

PREP TIME

COOK TIME

COOK TEMP

FREEZING

◯ yes ◯ no

SERVES

② ④ ⑥ ⑧ ⑩

DIFFICULTY

① ② ③ ④ ⑤

REVIEW

☆ ☆ ☆ ☆ ☆

VEGETARIAN ☐

DAIRY FREE ☐

LOW CARB ☐

GLUTEN FREE ☐

SUGAR FREE ☐

Notes:

Recipe 90:

PREP TIME

COOK TIME

COOK TEMP

FREEZING
◯ yes ◯ no

SERVES
② ④ ⑥ ⑧ ⑩

DIFFICULTY
① ② ③ ④ ⑤

REVIEW
☆ ☆ ☆ ☆ ☆

VEGETARIAN ☐
DAIRY FREE ☐
LOW CARB ☐
GLUTEN FREE ☐
SUGAR FREE ☐

Ingredients:

Directions:

Notes:

Recipe 91: _______________

PREP TIME

COOK TIME

COOK TEMP

FREEZING

◯ yes ◯ no

SERVES

② ④ ⑥ ⑧ ⑩

DIFFICULTY

① ② ③ ④ ⑤

REVIEW

☆ ☆ ☆ ☆ ☆

VEGETARIAN ☐
DAIRY FREE ☐
LOW CARB ☐
GLUTEN FREE ☐
SUGAR FREE ☐

Ingredients:

Directions:

Notes:

Recipe 92:

PREP TIME

COOK TIME

COOK TEMP

FREEZING

◯ yes ◯ no

SERVES

②　④　⑥　⑧　⑩

DIFFICULTY

①　②　③　④　⑤

REVIEW

☆ ☆ ☆ ☆ ☆

VEGETARIAN ☐
DAIRY FREE ☐
LOW CARB ☐
GLUTEN FREE ☐
SUGAR FREE ☐

Ingredients:

Directions:

Notes:

Recipe 93:

PREP TIME

COOK TIME

COOK TEMP

FREEZING

◯ yes   ◯ no

SERVES

② ④ ⑥ ⑧ ⑩

DIFFICULTY

① ② ③ ④ ⑤

REVIEW

☆ ☆ ☆ ☆ ☆

VEGETARIAN ☐
DAIRY FREE ☐
LOW CARB ☐
GLUTEN FREE ☐
SUGAR FREE ☐

Ingredients:

Directions:

Notes:

Recipe 94:

PREP TIME

COOK TIME

COOK TEMP

FREEZING

◯ yes   ◯ no

SERVES

② ④ ⑥ ⑧ ⑩

DIFFICULTY

① ② ③ ④ ⑤

REVIEW

☆ ☆ ☆ ☆ ☆

VEGETARIAN ☐

DAIRY FREE ☐

LOW CARB ☐

GLUTEN FREE ☐

SUGAR FREE ☐

Ingredients:

Directions:

Notes:

Recipe 95:

Ingredients:

Directions:

Notes:

Recipe 96: _______________

PREP TIME

COOK TIME

COOK TEMP

FREEZING

◯ yes   ◯ no

SERVES

② ④ ⑥ ⑧ ⑩

DIFFICULTY

① ② ③ ④ ⑤

REVIEW

☆ ☆ ☆ ☆ ☆

VEGETARIAN ☐

DAIRY FREE ☐

LOW CARB ☐

GLUTEN FREE ☐

SUGAR FREE ☐

Ingredients:

Directions:

Notes:

Recipe 97:

PREP TIME

COOK TIME

COOK TEMP

FREEZING

◯ yes   ◯ no

SERVES

② ④ ⑥ ⑧ ⑩

DIFFICULTY

① ② ③ ④ ⑤

REVIEW

☆ ☆ ☆ ☆ ☆

VEGETARIAN ☐

DAIRY FREE ☐

LOW CARB ☐

GLUTEN FREE ☐

SUGAR FREE ☐

Ingredients:

Directions:

Notes:

Recipe 98:

PREP TIME

COOK TIME

COOK TEMP

FREEZING

◯ yes   ◯ no

SERVES

② ④ ⑥ ⑧ ⑩

DIFFICULTY

① ② ③ ④ ⑤

REVIEW

☆ ☆ ☆ ☆ ☆

VEGETARIAN ☐

DAIRY FREE ☐

LOW CARB ☐

GLUTEN FREE ☐

SUGAR FREE ☐

Ingredients:

Directions:

Notes:

Recipe 99:

PREP TIME

COOK TIME

COOK TEMP

FREEZING

◯ yes　　◯ no

SERVES

② ④ ⑥ ⑧ ⑩

DIFFICULTY

① ② ③ ④ ⑤

REVIEW

☆ ☆ ☆ ☆ ☆

VEGETARIAN ☐

DAIRY FREE ☐

LOW CARB ☐

GLUTEN FREE ☐

SUGAR FREE ☐

Ingredients:

Directions:

Notes:

Recipe 100: _______________

PREP TIME

COOK TIME

COOK TEMP

FREEZING
◯ yes   ◯ no

SERVES
② ④ ⑥ ⑧ ⑩

DIFFICULTY
① ② ③ ④ ⑤

REVIEW
☆ ☆ ☆ ☆ ☆

VEGETARIAN ☐
DAIRY FREE ☐
LOW CARB ☐
GLUTEN FREE ☐
SUGAR FREE ☐

Ingredients:

Directions:

Notes:

Thank You

Please share your feedback on our book. Your opinion is very important to us. Thank you! Please let us know how you like our book at

 contact@georgicasworld.com